COFFEE WITH

to Savor

LYNN HOLLYN

ISBN: 0-8362-2165-6

Library of Congress Number: 96-83998

*P*ursuing beauty, the coffee cup imitates nature. I write this while admiring the randomly creeping stems of forget-me-nots in my garden. The tiny periwinkle blooms with sun-kissed centers are echoed in my china cup from Nana. Until she died a few years ago, she gave me a different floral china cup each Christmas. I set them out for my friends, and as we share coffee and conversation, Nana joins us. Coffee allows us to keep people, places, and things dear and near to us always.

One by one, like
a crocheted coverlet, my coffee
rituals lace together the moments
of my day. Most mornings, just before
dawn, the birds awaken me with their
cheerful greetings. Late summer brings a
cacophony of chatter; in the intense heat my
house wrens, bluebirds, robins, and sparrows
seem electrified. Today the morning mist lingers
in the valley. The rising fog is mirrored by
the steam in my coffeepot as I meander from
room to room, waiting for my perfect brew
to distill. It gives me a fine feeling
of contentment to be afoot in
the idle hour before the
world awakens.

I love to view the dawn from each room,
and my anticipation builds as the aroma
of coffee mixes with the scent of the
rosemary that grows on my windowsill.
With coffee I'm endowed with a dreamer's
freedom and a designer's perception.
Imagination in hand, I go forth with
passion to explore the universe and in so
doing to celebrate it. For it is in under-
standing one another and our world that
appreciation grows. In the morning,
with each dawn, coffee grants us a new
beginning. This is perhaps the drink's
most beguiling gift.

Sipping coffee begins an inner journey.
Often as not it then becomes a remembrance
or an anticipation of social gatherings to come.

As a symbol of hospitality, coffee
welcomes companionship into our home.
Like a longtime friend or a well-read book
it nurtures the seeds of kinship, comforts us
throughout the day, and warms us after the
fading of the sun. Even our nighttime dreams
give us glimpses of insight. Haven't we all
resolved a perplexing or troublesome issue in
our sleep, quite probably prompted by a late-
night cup of coffee?

offee weaves together the fabric of our lives. This invigorating brew is an invitation to conviviality and a shared communion of spirit and purpose. We resonate to its aroma. It beckons us from our hectic and fast-paced world to a place where encounters are unhurried, companionship is cherished, and the simplest pleasures leave us rejoicing.

The Old Coffee Shop

COFFEE

Coffee transcends words. It helps us make unspoken connections with the world around us. A loved one catches your eye over coffee and the morning newspaper. A nod and a smile are often the only exchange when your favorite shopkeeper prepares your cup just the way you like it. Loving glances at home and in the neighborhood are traded over our coffee.

Together the fabric of our lives of weaves the ligaments of our life into our traditions. Through our daily routines, we weave

Coffee lovers are inveterate gatherers. Like pickers of the beans, they carefully select words to accompany their brew. While taking tea is sometimes considered frivolous and an invitation to dally in trivia, coffee is inextricably linked to intellectual and business pursuits, as well as everyday life at home.

Coffee allows us
to share uncommon moments
with common folk throughout the world.
Over the years, sharing coffee has been a setting
for exchanges of friendship, love, intellectual discussion,
and daily trials and tribulations. These exchanges,
spurred by the stimulation and comfort of coffee,
draw us closer together and inspire us to
share our private thoughts. Coffee is
an enduring companion.

Before we moved west to California, my Swedish daughter reminisced with me about her first iced cappuccino at the Festival Cafe in New York. Coffee memories are already ingrained in my daughter. I need only mention delectable cappuccino, and her eyes sparkle and her mouth melts in a heartwarming smile. Familial love.

My mother's cup of coffee held a promise of everything.

We are bonded, mother and daughter, over coffee shared. I brewed a special blend today, and my mother said what I hope my daughter will one day say: "Let's just sit for a while with our coffee."

My coffee ritual often has the inviting charm of
a fanciful pastime. With friends expected, my daughter
and I set the table with our favorite faience and chinaware
and gather fresh blooms from the garden. We press our
finest linen napkins and lace-edged tablecloth, turning a
shared moment into a celebration. As surely as a flower
unfolds and a child grows, a party is planned.

Our place settings often reflect the seasons. In springtime, daffodils in eggcups nod to pansies on demitasse cups and saucers, like frocks tiered with petticoats and pinafores. Bunny napkin holders might scamper through this spring garden table as if Farmer McGregor had just hastened by. A touch of whimsy adds delight.

In summer, impatiens planted in espresso cups to be given as party favors is a special way to garnish the table. A frivolous assortment of flowered faience watering cans scattered with blooms and children's miniature coffeepots holding napkins complete the festive summer-garden theme.

Fall finds me lovingly restoring my earthenware to its popular position on the table. The hand-glazed coffeepot is nestled amid a runner of autumn leaves and a wreath of gourds. I fill it with persimmon bittersweet and let the late-afternoon light create patterns on my lustrous table. For a Halloween coffee séance, where we read one another's coffee grounds, I might carve individual coffeepot pumpkins and let them cast a warm if eerie glow.

In winter I succumb to white amaryllis and paper-whites. I create a fragrant, glittering, snow-swept tableau with chiffon and gold metallic netting scattered with crystal, vanilla candles, and pearls for a fireside coffee interlude.

In preparing for the quiet pleasures of a home-cooked meal for two, an elegant dinner party, or a family celebration, the cherished accessories we set out become just as enjoyable as the beverage itself. Like fine jewelry, bone china cups add luxury, the demitasse spoons add sparkle, the linen cloths layer us with softness, the lace trim adorns like the brooch on an Edwardian collar. Together with candlelight or sunlight, the table warms to the touch, feels luxurious to the hand, romances the eye. Indulge in the mellow glow as you begin your coffee ritual and let the drama unfold.

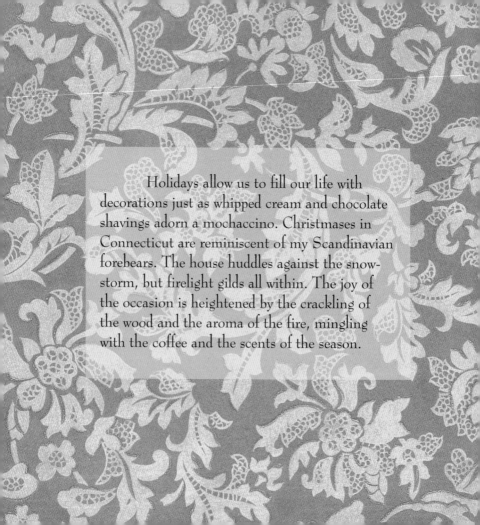

Holidays allow us to fill our life with decorations just as whipped cream and chocolate shavings adorn a mochaccino. Christmases in Connecticut are reminiscent of my Scandinavian forebears. The house huddles against the snowstorm, but firelight gilds all within. The joy of the occasion is heightened by the crackling of the wood and the aroma of the fire, mingling with the coffee and the scents of the season.

The secret of
the perfect cup of coffee
lies in the setting.

As a curtain of darkness falls
on Christmas night, memories will
linger in the coffee.

A proper coffee party for little girls begins with the porcelain server placed on a silver tray with hot water and Mom's finest china. Limoges is one of my daughter's favorites, along with a set I designed and hand-painted for her. She mixes in her own handmade, baked-clay coffee service. Heart-shaped shortbread cookies or powdered *kringle* are daintily arranged on lace doilies and ceremoniously brought to the miniature wicker table. This movable feast may be shared with Lady Lop-eared Rabbit, the Duchess of Salisbury, Gentleman Bear, the Honorable Duke of Kent, and the best friend of the hour.

*J*ust as the coffee ritual helps little girls become young ladies, it also eases boys into manhood. A fishing trip requires a steaming thermos of coffee as surely as does the boardroom. A young man will often test the feel of a masculine mug of black coffee in his hand. At first he might cringe at the bitterness of the scalding brew as it burns his tongue, but slowly he seeks the comfort in the taste and the settings in which it is consumed. This and many other rites of passage are spurred by the ritual of coffee.

Although coffee

is a renowned stimulant,

the coffee experience invites us to languish in

the moment, take a rest from the hectic day,

even write an unhurried note to a friend.

My desk is my little province.

I have chosen my pen, paper, blotter, and

paintings with care and surrounded myself with

flowers and other things that please me best.

Here is a place where, with my coffee,

silence is as well-loved as music,

solitude as well-loved as company.

Since the discovery of coffee, craftsmen and artisans have poured their genius into the design and invention of the beautiful accoutrements we use to prepare and partake of our cherished beverage. Sturdy roasters and grinders are fashioned of brass, silver, gold, and bronze. Romantic serving sets and delicate utensils are fashioned of copper, pewter, and silver. Dainty cups, saucers, creamers, and sugar bowls are molded of ivory porcelain or hand-crafted pottery. What makes the coffee setting so beautiful is not just the hand-painted cup with its caramel-colored liquid but the hue of the flowers, the sparkle of the silver, and all the other counterpoints in the tableau.

$\mathcal{R}$escued from the bins of flea markets and discovered amid attic clutter, coffee paraphernalia is enjoying a renaissance. As decorative elements alone or as charming vessels for flowers, spices, silver spoons, or other cherished mementos, coffee accessories are beautiful, versatile collectibles with a romantic heritage.

*P*orcelain is like an ocean stone worn smooth by the waters of time. China grows more beautiful, and its translucence increases with loving use. Create still lifes in your home that tell a story about your heritage. Let the table reflect the day's mood as you blend fond sentiments, family treasures, and traditions with your coffee.

Through porcelain, nature and coffee coalesce. Flowers and foliage often adorn our most beloved china. Coffee alfresco, in our gardens or on our patio, affords tranquillity—a seamless union of outdoors and indoors. From its humble roots on plantations to its elegant role as decoration on cups, coffee is intertwined with nature.

Cinnamon-Courage

Vanilla-Prosperity

Raspberry-Glory

Mint-Virtue

For each plant that
flavors coffee, I have
ascribed a sentiment to
enrich your own coffee
ritual or share its
meaning with a friend.
Why not pen a note in
calligraphy on a hand-
made paper card and
tuck it into a gift
of coffee beans secured
with raffia?

Nutmeg=
Good
Fortune

Strawberry=
Requited Love

Walnut=
Success

Cherry=Faithfulness

The beans from the coffee plant take on the characteristics of their surroundings; in them you taste the earth in which they grew, the air they inhaled, the water they drank, and the trees that shaded them. We might choose a pungent, earthy bean from the Djimmah region of Ethiopia; a bittersweet Mocha reminiscent of chocolate; a sweet Hawaiian Kona, nurtured near sugarcane and pineapple; or a peppery Mysore from India, land of spice and curry. These flavors reflect our moods or complement our menus.

Coffee is romantic, sensuous, and teeming with life. It is an adrenaline that fuels us, a magical elixir that inspires us. There are love stories within the fruit of the coffee plant. Normally two beans are nestled together,

nurtured, growing and
cultivated side by side.
Yet as with Romeo and
Juliet, they are harvested
together but then parted.
Our romantic imagination
is stimulated by stories
in literature of solitary
spirits like the rare single
coffee bean.

We taste with our eyes as well as our palate, and what could be more arousing than a visit to the local purveyor of coffee? The beans glisten, shiny and smooth, inviting you to fondle them in their rough-hewn burlap bags. The shop is a cornucopia of flavors and textures.

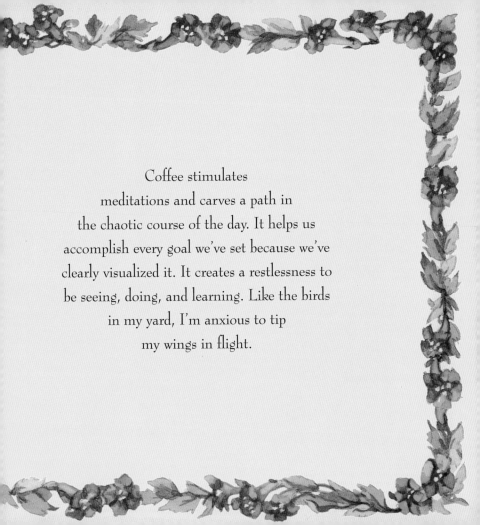

Coffee stimulates
meditations and carves a path in
the chaotic course of the day. It helps us
accomplish every goal we've set because we've
clearly visualized it. It creates a restlessness to
be seeing, doing, and learning. Like the birds
in my yard, I'm anxious to tip
my wings in flight.

In the midst of today's hectic living, there still exists a haven where we savor the simple and charming things in life. Our home is a perfect setting for comfort and special times. It is a sanctuary, a place where we can pamper ourselves, nurture our loved ones, and cultivate new friends. Coffee helps elevate everyday occurrences to special moments. Most of us have our own array of coffee memories at home that are forever in our hearts, no matter where we go.

Our hearts are filled with sweet nostalgia for the times when we viewed life's parade from our front porches. The verandah, receiving area for the warmth and sanctuary of the home, is a gathering place for family and friends. The setting is simple, with a wicker rocking chair or two, a footstool to hold a cup and saucer, a dim lantern that illuminates the screen door, and at dusk an orchestra of crickets and an audience of fireflies over the lawn.

The creaky porch swing
provides the most comfortable
seat for reading. Children
climb the gingerbread rails
and play on the painted steps;
neighbors stop by to visit.
And what better place for the
family to catch up
on the day's events?

The porch always welcomed us to contemplate events ahead or to meander with our morning coffee down pathways of thought we might never otherwise follow. In the afternoon green beans were snapped or corn was husked as the porch sheltered us from the sun. Our chores bonded us. Life was slower then, as twilight beckoned the family together. Late at night the conversation of generations filled the neighborhood as shooting stars fell from the sky.

y sitting room is a blend of porcelain, antique pine, and pillows in an inviting disarray to stimulate conversation. Cherished objects are set on all the tables, waiting to host a cup of coffee.

Coffee, of course, is merely the instrument. Silence and gathering our energies together can occur by using yoga, tai chi, prayer, cleaning, creativity, aerobics. These cleanse our mind, refresh us, and leave us lucid. Late in the afternoon when the sun slants shadows across my desk, I enjoy coffee time as did my ancestors. I gather my thoughts for one more spurt of creativity before supper. The ritual of the beverage and its invigorating properties is foreplay to the day and the night.

Artists, musicians, dancers, and writers have always captured the essence of coffee in our lives. Their gatherings in coffeehouses and salons, onstage and in back lots, inspired conversation and debate. Ideas were exchanged and examined, criticism and praise were offered, and the glories and difficulties of life were shared. Like multicolored threads woven into a fabric or brush strokes blended on a canvas, artisans imbue their work with ideas that were born with coffee.

I'm a fair-weather friend who casts aside the comforting cloak of my indoor rituals for the garden blooms and songs that beckon as winter's chill mantle dissolves into the earth. One of the earliest harbingers of spring, lilies of the valley shake sweet-smelling bells to arouse my senses. Coffee allows me to weed out thoughts and nurture dreams. Just as we make order out of chaos in nature by cultivating roses where tangled weeds once flourished, coffee creates clarity in our minds.

As I stroll through my garden
with loved ones and friends, we
admire new blooms of hollyhock,
evening primrose, and foxglove, each
one cultivated as gingerly as
friendships and traditions. We
breathe in the fragrance of lavender's
elusive perfume as it melds with the
aroma of vanilla in our coffee. In
the rare orchid plant that bestows
the rich vanilla flavoring I see that
my intuition is correct. Flowers and
coffee are inextricably linked.

In a few days I will move from my historic New England cottage to a California coastal setting, but I am still planting and weeding the garden for the stranger who will now own this land. I remember the cups of coffee shared and those sipped in solitude as I tended my seedlings or simply enjoyed their beauty. My brother would carry his cup as we took our morning stroll in the garden. Like doctors doing rounds we'd pluck a weed, deadhead a spent geranium, and discuss the diagnosis for the Japanese beetle flight. My children would rest with me after I did my spring planting. I am always learning from the musings inspired by my garden and my cup of coffee. I subscribe to Martin Luther's philosophy: *If I knew the world were to end tomorrow, I would plant an apple tree.*

*D*awn is celebrated alfresco in the garden. Surrounded by my English perennials—mallow, stokesia, toad lily, nicotiana, morning glory, and beds of forget-me-not—this spot is like blue-and-white porcelain touched by the glow of the sun's awakening. A ladybug alights on my hand-painted pansy faience mug as if Puck capriciously tossed them together on a midsummer's whim. With the morning star, day's messenger dancing from the east, come our first thoughts of coffee.

Do fairies
drink express
out of
Lady slippers or
honeysuckle cups?